Give Thanks!

Anytime Activities

By
Cindy Dingwall

Cover Illustration by
Dan Sharp

Inside Illustrations by
Anthony Carpenter

Publisher
In Celebration™
a division of Instructional Fair Group
Grand Rapids, Michigan 49544

About the Book

Give Thanks! is a book of puzzles and other activities that focus on the themes of Thanksgiving and of giving thanks. Each activity centers around a verse of thanksgiving. These verses and their accompanying activities encourage children to be thankful all year long.

Credits

Author: Cindy Dingwall
Cover Illustrator: Dan Sharp
Inside Illustrations: Anthony Carpenter
Project Director/Editor: Alyson Kieda
Editor: Meredith Van Zomeren
Graphic Layout: Deborah Hanson McNiff

About the Author

Cindy Dingwall has a degree in elementary education. She has worked as a day camp counselor, teacher, and children's librarian. Cindy has served on many church committees, taught Sunday school and VBS, and directed a children's choir. She has written 9 books and has been a contributing author to over 30 books of early childhood activities.

Standard Book Number: 0-7424-0019-0
Give Thanks! Anytime Activities

a division of Instructional Fair Group
a Tribune Education Company
3195 Wilson Drive NW
Grand Rapids, MI 49544

Filled with Blessings

Deuteronomy 28:2: "All these _ _ _ _ _ _ _ _ _ will come upon you . . . if you obey the LORD your God."

Connect the dots. Unscramble the word inside the cornucopia to complete the verse above. Draw pictures of things you are thankful for coming out of the cornucopia. Color the picture.

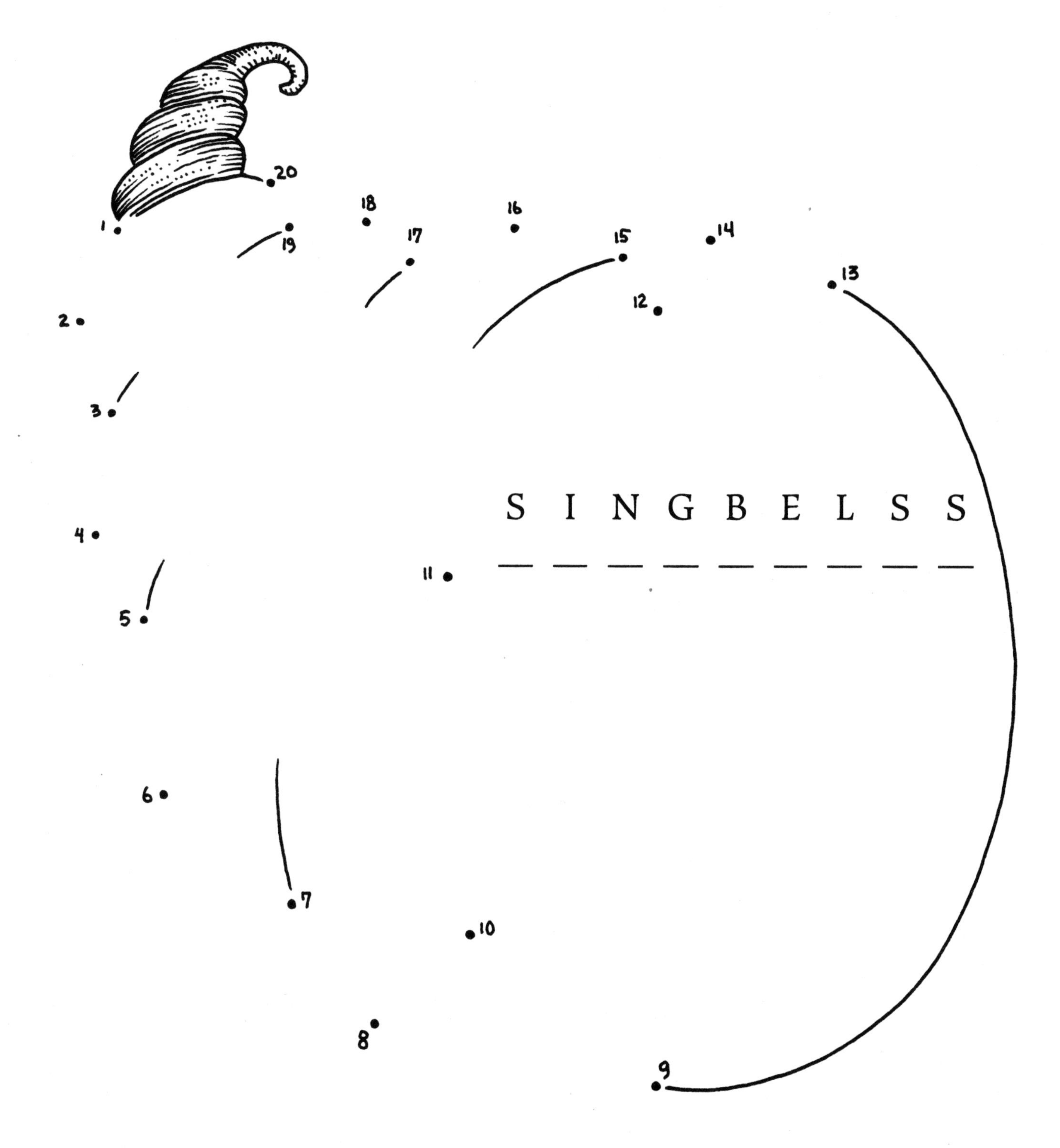

A Thank You Note

1 Chronicles 16:8: "Give thanks to the LORD, call on his name."

Write a thank you note to someone in your family. Tell your family member why you are thankful he or she is a part of your family.

Dear ______________________

Thank you for ______________________

____

____

____

____

____

____

____

____

____

Love,

____

Thanks Be to God

1 Chronicles 29:13: " _ _ _, _ _ _ _ _ _, _ _ _ _ _

_ _ _ _ _ _ _ _ _ _, _ _ _ _ _ _ _ _ _ _

_ _ _ _ _ _ _ _ _ _ _ _ _ _ _ _ _ _ _ _."

Circle every other word to discover what this verse says. Write the words in the blanks. Then draw a picture inside the frame of something or someone for which you are thankful.

LOVE GIVE CHURCH YOU FRIEND THANKS

FOOD AND CLOTHES PRAISE TOYS YOUR

BOOKS GLORIOUS SCHOOL NAME TEACHERS

NOW HOME OUR PETS GOD FAMILY WE

A Heart Filled with Love

Psalm 9:1 (RSV): "__ will give thanks __ __ the LORD with m__ __ __ __ __ __ __ __ __ __ __ __ __."

Use the picture clues to finish the verse. Write or draw what you are thankful for inside the heart.

Thank You, God

Psalm 25:10: "All the ways of the LORD are _ _ _ _ _ _ _ and faithful for those who keep the demands of his covenant."

Circle the letter where each set of words meet. Unscramble the letters to find the missing word.

BEFRIENDING
BEFRIENDING
FORGIVING
FORGIVING
HELPING
HELPING
MOLDING
MOLDING
STRENGTHENING
STRENGTHENING
TEACHING
TEACHING

Give Thanks

Psalm 30:12: "O Lord m__ God, __ will give __ __ __ thanks __ __ __ever."

Use the picture clues to decipher this verse. Then color the picture.

A Poem of Thanksgiving

Psalm 52:9 (RSV): "I will thank you forever, because of what you have done."

On a scrap sheet of paper, create an original Thanksgiving poem. Then write and illustrate it below.

Thanksgiving Fun

Psalm 69:30: "I will praise God's name in song and glorify him with thanksgiving."

How many words can you make using the letters in the word *thanksgiving*? Write them below.

THANKSGIVING

A Code of Thanks

Psalm 75:1

Use the following code to decipher this verse.

1 = A	7 = G	12 = L	17 = Q	22 = V
2 = B	8 = H	13 = M	18 = R	23 = W
3 = C	9 = I	14 = N	19 = S	24 = X
4 = D	10 = J	15 = O	20 = T	25 = Y
5 = E	11 = K	16 = P	21 = U	26 = Z
6 = F				

“ 23 5   7 9 22 5   20 8 1 14 11 19   20 15

25 15 21,   15   7 15 4 . . .   6 15 18   25 15 21 18

14 1 13 5   9 19   14 5 1 18.”

Let's Go to Church

Psalm 100:2: "Worship the LORD with gladness."

Oh no! Road construction! Help the family find a different way to church on Thanksgiving Day.

Say That Again!

Psalm 100:4

Color the Z's brown. The leftover letters spell out the first part of the verse. Then unscramble the letters coming out of the cornucopia to complete the verse.

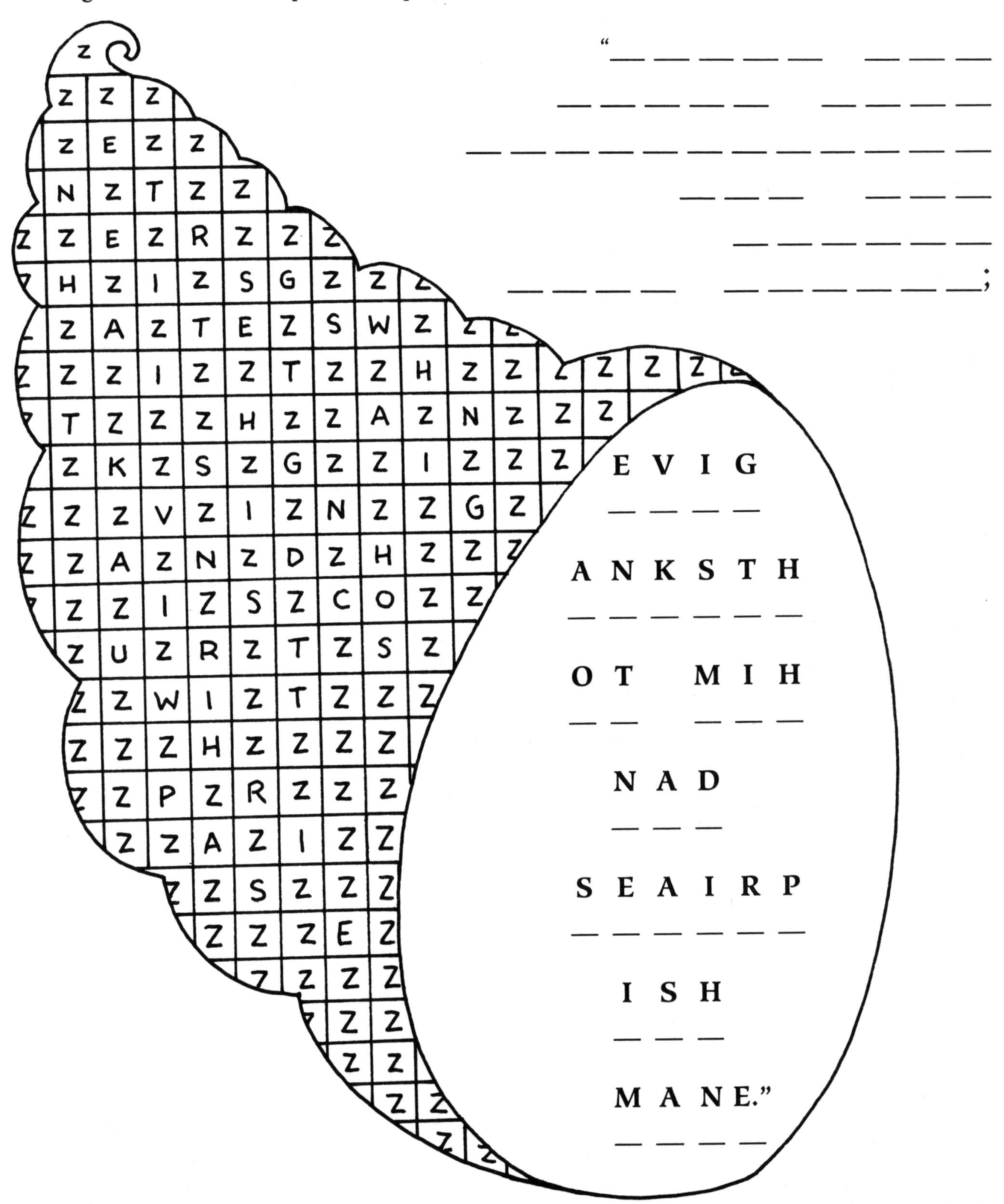

What's the Message?

Psalm 105:1: "_ _ _ _   _ _ _ _ _ _ _ _   _ _   _ _ _   _ _ _ _ _."

Circle or cross out the following words. (Some letters will be used more than once.) The leftover letters will spell out the verse. Write it in the blanks above.

God	food	prayers	teacher
fun	enter	come	welcome
message	VBS	Lord	Jesus
love	Sunday	games	music
pastor	school		

S	M	E	S	S	A	G	E	L	G
U	U	J	E	S	U	S	W	O	I
N	S	V	P	R	A	Y	E	R	S
D	I	E	A	T	H	F	L	D	T
A	C	A	S	N	K	O	C	G	E
Y	S	T	T	O	T	O	O	A	A
S	C	H	O	O	L	D	M	M	C
G	F	V	R	C	O	M	E	E	H
O	U	B	H	E	V	L	O	S	E
D	N	S	R	D	E	N	T	E	R

Thanksgiving Turkey

Psalm 128:2

Unscramble the words inside each feather. (*Hint:* They are all fruits.) Starting at the bottom left-hand feather, print the circled letters in the spaces below to complete the verse.

Say It!

Jeremiah 31:12: "Rejoice in the _ _ _ _ _ _ _ of the LORD."

Fill in the missing letters to complete each word below. The letters in the box will spell out a message. Then use the circled letters to complete the verse above.

A Family Thanksgiving

Daniel 2:23: "I thank and praise you, O God of my fathers."

Draw a picture of you and your family giving thanks to God.

God Provides

Matthew 7:7: "Ask and it will be given to you; seek and you will find; knock and the door will be opened to you."

God hears us when we pray. Can you find your way to Jesus?

Sharing: A Way to Say Thanks

Matthew 25:35: "For I was hungry and you gave me something to eat, I was thirsty and you gave me something to drink."

On the bag, draw pictures of the groceries you would buy for a needy person. Perhaps you and your parents could take a real bag of groceries to a food pantry.

Be Thankful for Your Family

Mark 5:19: "Go home to your family and tell them how much the Lord has done for you, and how he has had mercy on you."

Write the names of your family members in the spaces below. Next to each family member's name, list some of the things he or she does for which you are thankful.

NAME	THANK YOU FOR

Feeding the Hungry

Mark 8:6–7: "When he had taken the seven loaves and _ _ _ _ _ _ _ _ _ _ _ _ _ _, he broke them and gave them to his disciples to set before the people, and they did so."

Follow the letter path to discover the words missing in the verse.

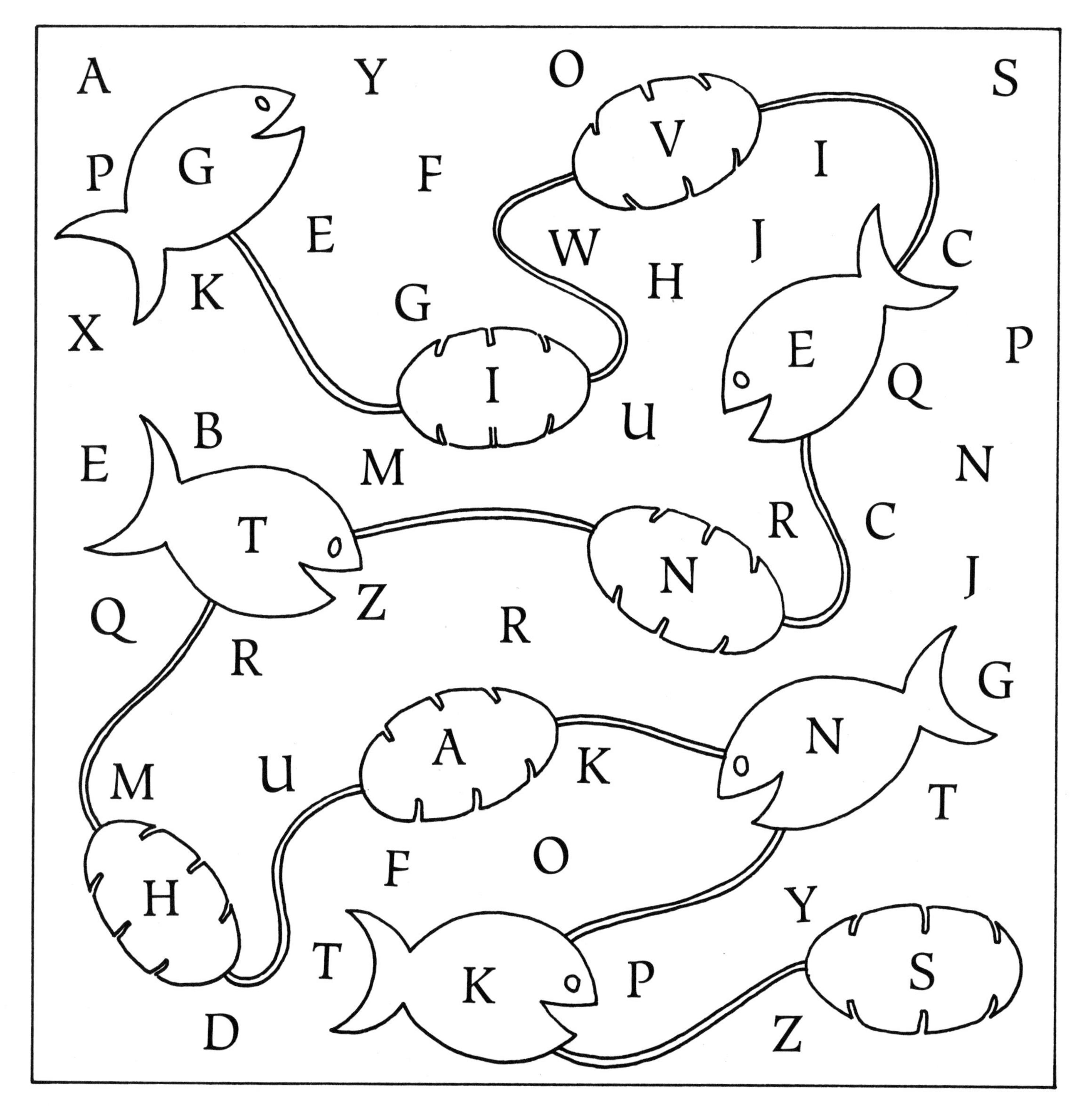

Which Way Are You Going?

Romans 7:25: "_ _ _ _ _ _ _ _ _ _ _ _ _ _—
_ _ _ _ _ _ _ _ _ _ _ _ _ _ _ _ _ _ _ _ _ _ _ _ _ _ _ _ _ _!"

Circle every other word. Print those words in the spaces above. Use the rest of the words to complete the verse. *(Hint:* Use a mirror or hold the paper backwards and read the message.) Then draw and color a picture of your favorite place. Thank God for it.

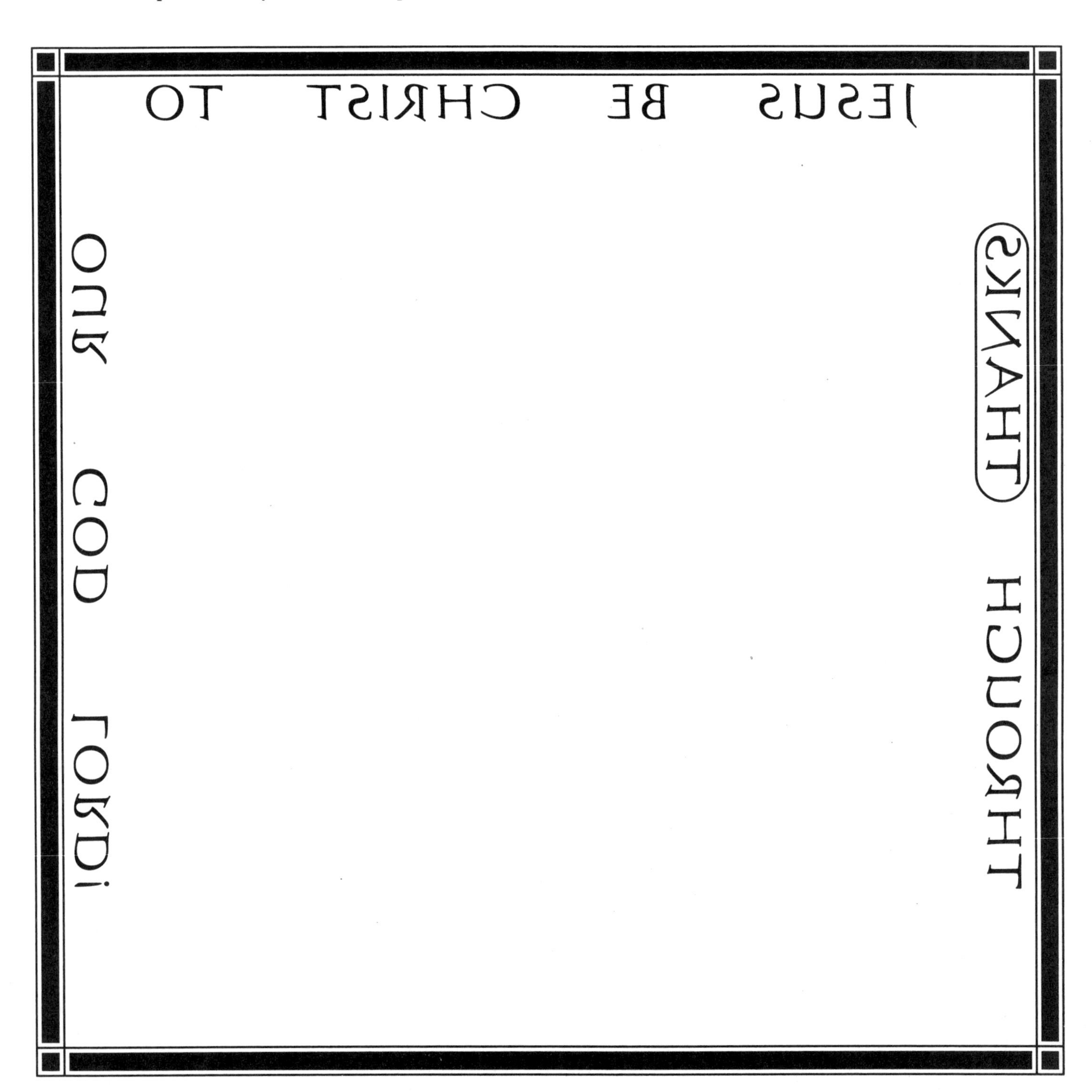

Family Pictures

Romans 14:6: "He who regards one day as special, does so to the Lord. He who eats meat, eats to the Lord, for he gives thanks to God."

Draw a picture of your family enjoying their Thanksgiving celebration.

What Does God Give?

1 Corinthians 15:57: "But thanks be to God! He gives us the _ _ _ _ _ _ _ through our Lord Jesus Christ."

Color: 1 = Yellow, 2 = Orange, 3 = Red, 4 = Blue, 5 = Green, 6 = Purple, 7 = Pink

Thanksgiving Litany

2 Corinthians 9:15: "Thanks be to God for his indescribable gift!"

Write a litany that thanks God for the blessings in your life. Say it together with your family. You say the first line. Let your family respond with "Thanks be to God for his indescribable gift!"

Thank you, God, for the gift of ______________________________!

Thanks be to God for his indescribable gift!

Thank you, God, for the gift of ______________________________!

Thanks be to God for his indescribable gift!

Thank you, God, for the gift of ______________________________!

Thanks be to God for his indescribable gift!

Thank you, God, for the gift of ______________________________!

Thanks be to God for his indescribable gift!

Thank you, God, for the gift of ______________________________!

Thanks be to God for his indescribable gift!

Thank you, God, for the gift of ______________________________!

Thanks be to God for his indescribable gift!

Thank you, God, for the gift of ______________________________!

Thanks be to God for his indescribable gift!

What Did You Say?

Use your Bible to complete the crossword puzzle on page 27. Unscramble the letters inside each set of shapes and print them in the correct spaces below.

○ ___ ___ ___ ___ △ ___ ___ ___ ___ ___ ___ ___ ◇ ___ ___

□ ___ ___ ___ ▽ ___ ___ ___ ___! (1 Chronicles 16:8)

DOWN:

1. "Now, our God, we give you thanks, and praise your _____ name" (1 Chronicles 29:13).
2. "I was hungry and you gave me something to eat. I was _____ and you gave me something to drink" (Matthew 25:35).
3. "All these _____ will come upon you" (Deuteronomy 28:2).
4. "Worship the LORD with _____" (Psalm 100:2).
5. "I praise you, O LORD, with all my _____" (Psalm 9:1).

ACROSS:

1. "We give thanks to you, O _____" (Psalm 75:1).
2. "Thanks be to God—through _____ Christ our Lord" (Romans 7:25).
3. "Enter his gates with _____ and his courts with praise; give thanks to him and praise his name" (Psalm 100:4).
4. "Rejoice in the _____ of the LORD" (Jeremiah 31:12).
5. "Give _____ to the LORD, call on his name" (1 Chronicles 16:8).

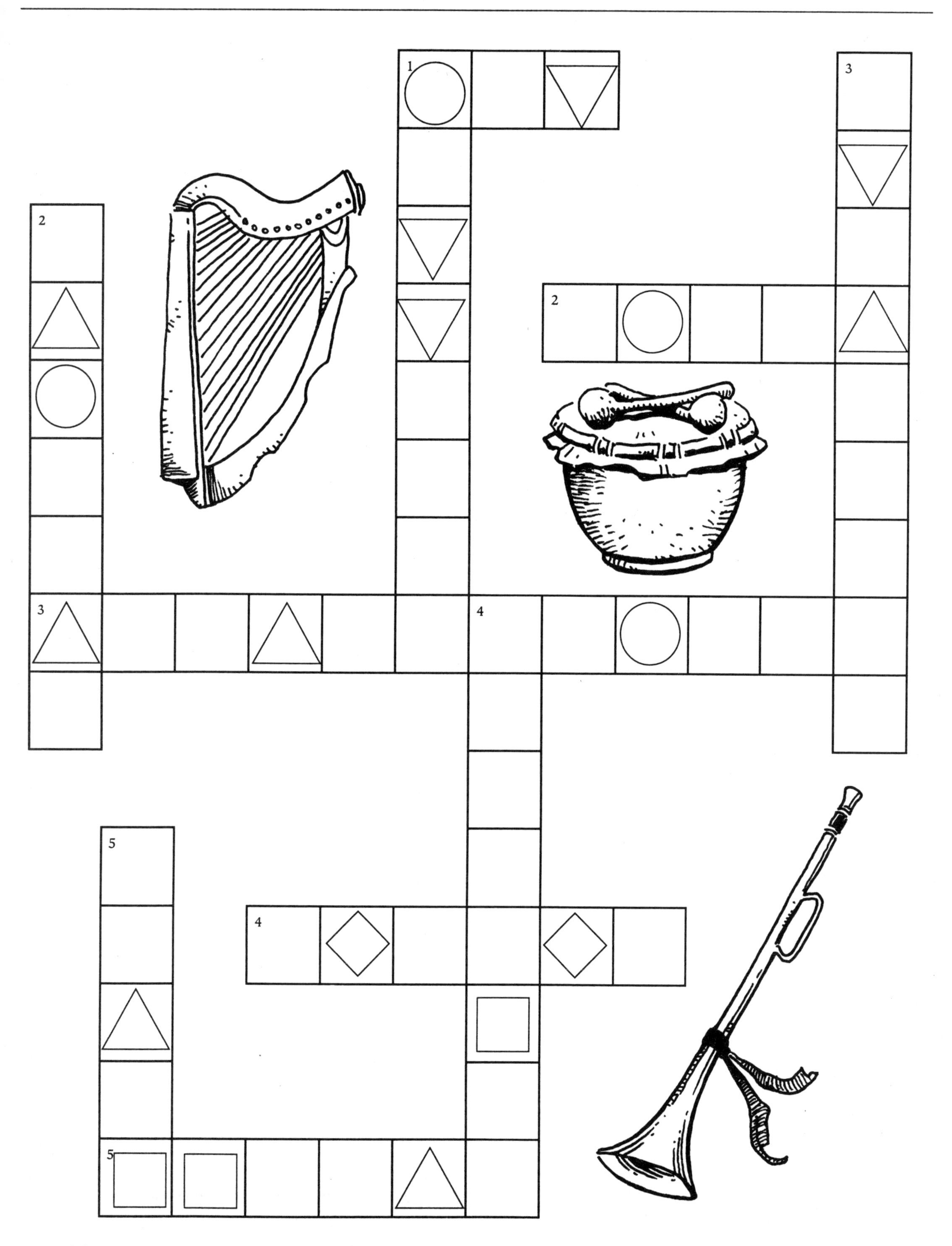

1
3
2
2
3
4
5
4
5

Thanksgiving Story

Write a Thanksgiving story. Give it a title and illustrate it below.

Thanksgiving to God

2 Corinthians 9:11: "You will be made rich in every way so that you can be generous on every occasion, and through us your generosity will result in thanksgiving to God."

The word *thanksgiving* is written below. Write one or more persons, places, or things you are thankful for after each letter. Each person, place, and thing must begin with that letter.

T
H
A
N
K
S
G
I
V
I
N
G

Prayer of Thanksgiving

1 Timothy 2:1: "I urge, then, first of all, that requests, prayers, intercession and thanksgiving be made for everyone."

Trace around your hand or ask someone to trace it for you on the sheet below. Write a prayer of thanks on the hand.

Can You Find It?

Hebrews 4:13: "Nothing in all creation is hidden from God's sight."

Can you find and color all of these hidden things?: cornucopia, pumpkin, apple, corn, squash, pie, fork, and spoon.

Answer Key

page 13

Say That Again!

Psalm 100:4

Color the Z's brown. The leftover letters spell out the first part of the verse. Then unscramble the letters coming out of the cornucopia to complete the verse.

page 14

What's the Message?

Psalm 105:1: "Give thanks to the Lord."

Circle or cross out the following words. (Some letters will be used more than once.) The leftover letters will spell out the verse. Write it in the blanks above.

God	food	prayers	teacher
fun	enter	come	welcome
message	VBS	Lord	Jesus
love	Sunday	games	music
pastor	school		

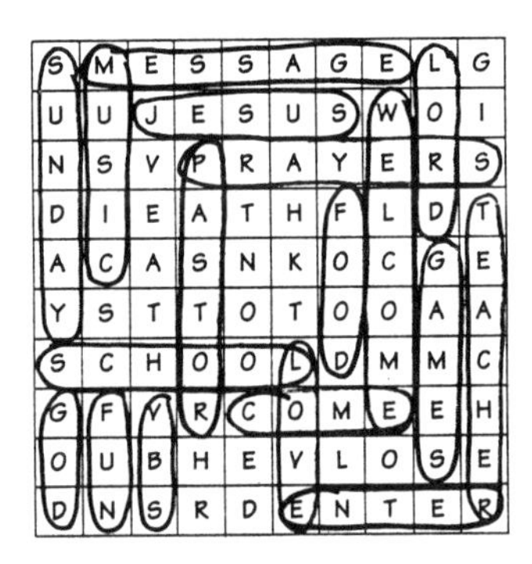

page 15

Thanksgiving Turkey

Psalm 128:2

Unscramble the words inside each feather. (*Hint:* They are all fruits.) Starting at the bottom left-hand feather, print the circled letters in the spaces below to complete the verse.

page 16

Say It!

Jeremiah 31:12: "Rejoice in the bounty of the LORD."

Fill in the missing letters to complete each word below. The letters in the box will spell out a message, then use the circled letters to complete the verse above.

page 26

What Did You Say?

Use your Bible to complete the crossword puzzle on page 27. Unscramble the letters inside each set of shapes and print them in the correct spaces below.

○Give △thanks ◇to

□the ▽Lord! (1 Chronicles 16:8)

DOWN:

1. "Now, our God, we give you thanks, and praise your _____ name" (1 Chronicles 29:13).
2. "I was hungry and you gave me something to eat. I was _____ and you gave me something to drink" (Matthew 25:35).
3. "All these _____ will come upon you" (Deuteronomy 28:2).
4. "Worship the LORD with _____" (Psalm 100:2).
5. "I praise you, O LORD, with all my _____" (Psalm 9:1).

ACROSS:

1. "We give thanks to you, O _____" (Psalm 75:1).
2. "Thanks be to God—through _____ Christ our Lord" (Romans 7:25).
3. "Enter his gates with _____ and his courts with praise; give thanks to him and praise his name" (Psalm 100:4).
4. "Rejoice in the _____ of the LORD" (Jeremiah 31:12).
5. "Give _____ to the LORD, call on his name" (1 Chronicles 16:8).

page 27

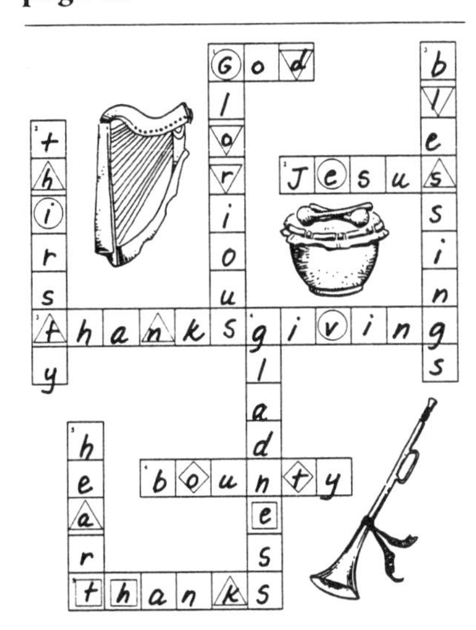

page 31

Can You Find It?

Hebrews 4:13: "Nothing in all creation is hidden from God's sight."

Can you find and color all of these hidden things?: cornucopia, pumpkin, apple, corn, squash, pie, fork, and spoon.